EVERYTHING WOMEN KNOW ABOUT MEN

10085023

EVERYTHING WOMEN KNOW ABOUT MEN

EVERYTHING WOMEN KNOW ABOUT MEN

EVERYTHING WOMEN KNOW ABOUT MEN

EVERYTHING WOMEN KNOW ABOUT MEN

EVERYTHING WOMEN KNOW ABOUT MEN

EVERYTHING WOMEN KNOW ABOUT MEN

EVERYTHING WOMEN KNOW ABOUT MEN

EVERYTHING WOMEN KNOW ABOUT MEN

EVERYTHING WOMEN KNOW ABOUT MEN

EVERYTHING WOMEN KNOW ABOUT MEN

EVERYTHING WOMEN KNOW ABOUT MEN

EVERYTHING WOMEN KNOW ABOUT MEN

EVERYTHING WOMEN KNOW ABOUT MEN

EVERYTHING WOMEN KNOW ABOUT MEN

EVERYTHING WOMEN KNOW ABOUT MEN

EVERYTHING WOMEN KNOW ABOUT MEN

EVERYTHING WOMEN KNOW ABOUT MEN

EVERYTHING WOMEN KNOW ABOUT MEN

EVERYTHING WOMEN KNOW ABOUT MEN

EVERYTHING WOMEN KNOW ABOUT MEN

EVERYTHING WOMEN KNOW ABOUT MEN

EVERYTHING WOMEN KNOW ABOUT MEN

www.ingramcontent.com/pod-product-compliance
Lightning Source LLC
Chambersburg PA
CBHW031514040426
42445CB00009B/225

* 9 7 8 0 9 7 6 4 8 8 2 0 0 *